SP
394.26
DEA

3 24571 0901488 0
Dean, Sheri.

Memorial Day

$11.26

DATE DUE	BORROWER'S NAME	ROOM NO.

SP
394.26
DEA

3 24571 0901488 0
Dean, Sheri.

Memorial Day

WEEKLY WR READER

EARLY LEARNING LIBRARY

Our Country's Holidays/
Las fiestas de nuestra nación

Memorial Day/
Día de los Caídos
by/por Sheri Dean

Reading consultant/Consultora de lectura:
Susan Nations, M.Ed.,
author/literacy coach/consultant in literacy development
autora/tutora de alfabetización/
consultora de desarrollo de la lectura

Please visit our web site at: www.earlyliteracy.cc
For a free color catalog describing Weekly Reader® Early Learning Library's list
of high-quality books, call 1-877-445-5824 (USA) or 1-800-387-3178 (Canada).
Weekly Reader® Early Learning Library's fax: (414) 336-0164.

Library of Congress Cataloging-in-Publication Data available upon request from publisher.
Fax (414) 336-0157 for the attention of the Publishing Records Department.

ISBN 0-8368-6521-9 (lib. bdg.)
ISBN 0-8368-6528-6 (softcover)

This edition first published in 2006 by
Weekly Reader® Early Learning Library
A Member of the WRC Media Family of Companies
330 West Olive Street, Suite 100
Milwaukee, WI 53212 USA

Copyright © 2006 by Weekly Reader® Early Learning Library

Managing editor: Valerie J. Weber
Art direction: Tammy West
Cover design and page layout: Kami Strunsee
Picture research: Cisley Celmer
Translators: Tatiana Acosta and Guillermo Gutiérrez

Picture credits: Cover, © A. Ramey/PhotoEdit; p. 5 © Skjold Photographs; p. 7
© Otis Imboden/National Geographic Image Collection; pp. 9, 11, 13, 15 © AP/Wide
World Photos; p. 17 © Tom Prettyman/PhotoEdit; p. 19 © David Young-Wolff/PhotoEdit;
p. 21 © Joe Raedle/Getty Images

Printed in the United States of America

1 2 3 4 5 6 7 8 9 10 09 08 07 06

Note to Educators and Parents

Reading is such an exciting adventure for young children! They are beginning to integrate their oral language skills with written language. To encourage children along the path to early literacy, books must be colorful, engaging, and interesting; they should invite the young reader to explore both the print and the pictures.

In *Our Country's Holidays*, children learn how the holidays they celebrate in their families and communities are observed across our nation. Using lively photographs and simple prose, each title explores a different national holiday and explains why it is significant.

Each book is specially designed to support the young reader in the reading process. The familiar topics are appealing to young children and invite them to read — and reread — again and again. The full-color photographs and enhanced text further support the student during the reading process.

In addition to serving as wonderful picture books in schools, libraries, homes, and other places where children learn to love reading, these books are specifically intended to be read within an instructional guided reading group. This small group setting allows beginning readers to work with a fluent adult model as they make meaning from the text. After children develop fluency with the text and content, the book can be read independently. Children and adults alike will find these books supportive, engaging, and fun!

— Susan Nations, M.Ed., author, literacy coach,
and consultant in literacy development

Nota para los maestros y los padres

¡Leer es una aventura tan emocionante para los niños pequeños! A esta edad están comenzando a integrar su manejo del lenguaje oral con el lenguaje escrito. Para animar a los niños en el camino de la lectura incipiente, los libros deben ser coloridos, estimulantes e interesantes; deben invitar a los jóvenes lectores a explorar la letra impresa y las ilustraciones.

Con la serie *Las fiestas de nuestra nación* los jóvenes lectores aprenderán que las fiestas que sus familias y sus comunidades celebran son días especiales en todo el país. Mediante vistosas fotografías y textos sencillos, cada libro explora una fiesta nacional diferente y explica por qué es importante.

Cada libro está especialmente diseñado para ayudar a los jóvenes lectores en el proceso de lectura. Los temas familiares llaman la atención de los niños y los invitan a leer — y releer — una y otra vez. Las fotografías a todo color y el tamaño de la letra ayudan aún más al estudiante en el proceso de lectura.

Además de servir como maravillosos libros ilustrados en escuelas, bibliotecas, hogares y otros lugares donde los niños aprenden a amar la lectura, estos libros han sido especialmente concebidos para ser leídos en un grupo de lectura guiada. Este contexto permite que los lectores incipientes trabajen con un adulto que domina la lectura mientras van determinando el significado del texto. Una vez que los niños dominan el texto y el contenido, el libro puede ser leído de manera independiente. ¡Estos libros les resultarán útiles, estimulantes y divertidos a niños y a adultos por igual!

— Susan Nations, M.Ed., autora/tutora de alfabetización/
consultora de desarrollo de la lectura

On Memorial Day, we think about people who died for our country.

- - - - - - - - - - - - - - - - - -

El Día de los Caídos recordamos a las personas que han muerto por nuestro país.

These people fought on land, on the seas, and in the air. They all wore different uniforms. They all tried to keep our country safe.

Estas personas lucharon en tierra, mar y aire. Llevaban distintos uniformes. Todos trataron de proteger nuestro país.

Memorial Day is always on the last Monday in May. Many flowers bloom in May. We often use flowers to honor people who died for our country.

El Día de los Caídos se celebra siempre el último lunes de mayo. En mayo se abren muchas flores. A menudo, usamos flores para honrar a las personas que murieron por nuestro país.

On Memorial Day, we put flowers on rivers, lakes, and seas. The flowers honor sailors who died at sea. We also put flowers and flags on graves.

El Día de los Caídos, echamos flores en los ríos, los lagos y los mares. Las flores son un homenaje a los marineros que murieron en el mar. También ponemos flores y banderas en las tumbas.

10

We buy red paper flowers. We wear the flowers to honor our soldiers and sailors.

———————————————————————————

Compramos flores de papel rojas. Nos ponemos estas flores para honrar a nuestros soldados y marineros.

People fly flags halfway down the flagpole to honor people who have died. Putting the flag like this is called half-mast.

——————————————————————

La gente cuelga las banderas a mitad del asta para honrar a los caídos. Esto se llama izar la bandera a media asta.

15

Many people watch parades. Soldiers, sailors, and other groups march in the parades.

Mucha gente va a ver los desfiles. Soldados, marineros y otros grupos marchan en los desfiles.

16

On Memorial Day, we think about family and friends who died for our country.

El Día de los Caídos pensamos en los familiares y amigos que murieron por nuestro país.

On Memorial Day, we take a minute to be silent. We often pray for world peace.

El Día de los Caídos guardamos un minuto de silencio. Con frecuencia, rezamos por la paz mundial.

Glossary

flagpole — a pole from which a flag flies

graves — places where people are buried

half-mast — a point about halfway down from the top of a flagpole

Glosario

asta — palo donde se coloca la bandera

media asta — punto medio del asta de la bandera

tumbas — lugares donde se entierra a las personas

For More Information/ Más información

Books

Let's Get Ready for Memorial Day. Lloyd Douglas (Sagebrush)
Memorial Day Surprise. Theresa Martin Golding
 (Boyds Mills Press)

Libros

El día de los caídos. Mir Tamim Ansary (Heinemann)

Web Sites/Páginas web

Memorial Day
Día de los Caídos
www.patriotism.org/memorial_day/index.html
Learn about the history of the holiday and how we honor those
who help our country.
Conoce la historia de esta fiesta nacional y cómo honramos a
quienes ayudan a nuestro país.

Index

Índice

About the Author

Sheri Dean is a school librarian in Milwaukee, Wisconsin. She was an elementary school teacher for fourteen years. She enjoys introducing books and information to curious children and adults.

Información sobre la autora

Sheri Dean trabaja como bibliotecaria en Milwaukee, Wisconsin. Durante catorce años, fue maestra de primaria. A Sheri le gusta proporcionar información y libros novedosos a niños y adultos con ganas de aprender.